Luke 2:52

Creepy Creatures
& Bizarre Beasts
From the Bible

Creepy Creatures & Bizarre Beasts
from the Bible

by Rick Osborne & Ed Strauss

zonder**kidz**

ZONDERVAN.COM/
AUTHOR**TRACKER**

ZONDERKIDZ

Creepy Creatures & Bizarre Beasts from the Bible
Copyright 2004 by Lightwave Publishing, Inc.

Requests for information should be addressed to:
Zonderkidz, Grand Rapids, Michigan 49530

ISBN 978-0-310-70654-0

Library of Congress Cataloging-in-Publication Data
Osborne, Rick.
Creepy creatures & bizarre beasts from the Bible / Rick Osborne & Ed Strauss
           p. cm.
Summary: A light-hearted look at the animals of the Bible, from those of Noah's ark to sacrificial
bulls, and what their stories reveal about God and our relationship with Him.
          ISBN 0-310-70654-8
1. Animals in the Bible—Juvenile literature. 2. Children—Conduct of life. [1. Animals in the Bible. 2.
Conduct of life.] I. Title: Creepy creatures and bizarre beasts from the Bible. II. Strauss, Ed, 1953- III.
Title.
BS663 .O83 2004
220.8'59—dc21   2002155616

Editor: Gwen Ellis
Interior Art Direction: Michelle Lenger
Interior Illustrations: Anthony Carpenter
Cover illustration: Erwin Haya
Design & Cover Direction: Merit Alderink

Printed in U.S.A.

contents

INTRODUCTION

The Bible goes on and on about people—but there are more living things on earth and in other realms than just humans. Fortunately! Think how boring it would be if there were no Venus flytraps gobbling flies, no duck-billed platypuses doing whatever they do, and no four-faced creatures to scare the absolute willies out of you.

This book talks about nearly every animal, beast, and amazing creature mentioned in the Bible. We even cover a few exceptional plants that talk.

We also talk about incredible beasts that don't actually exist—such as four-headed leopards, lions with wings, horses that breathe out fire, unicorns, and even dragons. You know, amazing creatures from visions and dreams, that kind of thing.

There are cool stories about some amazing beasts and creatures in the Bible, and you'll have a blast reading about them. You'll probably learn some stuff as well. God made animals and he uses them not only to provide food for us and to play their part in the world, but also to help us understand more about him. He once made a donkey talk in order to teach Balaam a lesson.

Solomon was one of the smartest guys ever, and God taught him lessons from eagles, snakes, lions, ants, and even rock badgers. Even the fantastic imaginary or symbolic creatures in the Bible that came from God's amazing imagination are there to teach us. So enjoy the greatest parade of amazing creatures since Noah's Ark!

BIBLE ANIMALS

And God Created Animals

Why did God create animals? The Bible says, "Thou hast created all things, and for thy pleasure they are and were created" (Revelation 4:11, KJV). Everything that exists is here to give God pleasure. So animals please God. He thinks they're cool. That's why they're here.

You've heard of the Animal Kingdom, right? Do you know who was the first king of the beasts? Not some lion. It was Adam. God told him, "Rule over the fish of the sea and the birds of the air and over every living creature that moves on the ground" (Genesis 1:28).

Ruling over animals does not mean being a

dictator. God wants us to be kind to animals. Proverbs 12:10 says, "A righteous man cares for the needs of his animal." In Isaiah 40:11 God described a good shepherd: "He gathers the lambs in his arms and carries them close to his heart; he gently leads those that have young." In fact, when the Israelites rested on the Sabbath, God insisted they give the animals a day off too (Deuteronomy 5:14). Time out, ox! Siesta, donkey!

But you can't take that too far. When someone insists, "Animals are people too," they're saying that animals have as many rights as people and you should only eat vegetables—because to eat meat you need to kill animals. God said in Genesis 9:3, "Everything that lives and moves will be food for you. Just as I gave you the green plants, I now give you everything."

See, some people think animals are just as important as people. Animals are very important and God cares for them, but they were not created to be God's very own children like we were. But God did create them to help his children. They help keep the world working, they keep us company, help us get around, help us enjoy God's creation, and provide us with food. That's important stuff. Don't set a place at the table for your dog, but treat him well and enjoy him a lot.

noah's ark— floating zoo

When you talk Bible animals there's one story that always goes right to the head of the line: Noah and the ark. You've probably seen dozens of different Noah books ever since you were old enough to chew on them, but here are some facts you're only now ready for.

First of all, artists almost always draw the ark wrong. You've probably got this picture stuck in

your head of an elephant and a giraffe smiling as they stand on top of some curvy little boat. Bwaaaaappp! Wrong! The ark was a huge rectangular box 450 feet long, 75 feet wide, and 45 feet high (Genesis 6:15). The animals were not up on the deck and they were not smiling. At least Noah wasn't smiling. You'll see why in a minute.

Before the gross stuff, this announcement: animals have a purpose on earth. God cares for them. If he didn't care, he wouldn't have had Noah work 120 years to build an ark to save them. He'd have just told Noah to get on a houseboat with a bunch of chickens. "There, that'll do ya." But no, God told him to bring two of all living creatures into the ark. This included critters like skunks, vultures, and howler mon-

keys that Noah might have been tempted to leave behind. Noah also brought seven of every clean animal (Genesis 6:19; 7:2).

The ark was divided into three levels, lower, middle, and upper decks (Genesis 6:16). Probably heavy animals like elephants and hippos were on the bottom deck so the boat wouldn't tip over. The sheep, deer, and middle-sized animals were on the middle deck and the birds and rabbits and skunks and termites and ants were on the top deck.

Now for gross facts:

• **Fact one: Noise!** Every day, all day long, was like being trapped in an old Tarzan movie with the volume turned up high. (There were howler monkeys.) For one full year it was feeding time at the zoo. With all those cramped, small rooms the echo must have been maddening.

• **Fact two: It was dark.** Maybe Noah had a grating system that let in light from above, but it was still dim. Electric lights hadn't been invented so Noah couldn't just flip a switch if he wanted to inspect the basement of the ark. Plus, he had to be careful with lamps or he'd burn the ark down. (It was made of pitch-covered wood, remember?) SHEM: Dad, are we in the carnivore section yet? NOAH: Oh yeah. Look at all them glowing, lightbulb eyes.

• **Fact three: The ark stunk**—and I mean really, really stunk! It was raining nonstop so God told Noah to build one super-long window, 18 inches high, that ran along the whole top of the ark (Genesis 6:16). An overhanging roof kept the rain out. The window let in air, but don't tell me Noah and his sons weren't gagging with the smell of several hundred thousand hot, wet, stinking, furry animals. Ever visited or driven by a farm?

• **Fact four: Animals poop.** The bigger they are, the more they poop. What? You think they held it till they got off the ark? No way. Probably half Noah's day was spent shoveling up tons of species feces and dumping it out poop-chutes into the ocean. And with the ocean heaving and the floor slippery, probably every day one of Noah's boys slipped and slid in the slimy sludge. (This isn't where the term "poop deck" came from.)

• **Fact five: Animals pee.** This is not the kind of stuff you can scoop up in a shovel. And it didn't just soak into the floorboards. God made sure of that when he had Noah waterproof the ark. So, this pee wasn't going anywhere. It probably sloshed around like a yellow riptide every time the ark tilted. So, like, how did they deal with it? I don't know. And frankly I don't like to think about it.

(Okay, okay, if you just can't sleep until you figure this one out, Noah probably had a drainage system—little ditches in the floor to carry the urine away. But still ... ever smell a public bathroom with pee all over it?)

We could tell you more gross stuff about the ark, but this has probably been enough to destroy your baby-book idea of a giraffe and elephant smiling.

Get Smarter

When Noah said yes to God he made a commitment to take care of a whole shipload of pets for God. He took the good with the bad and did a great job. If you have a pet and you promised your parents you'd take care of it, make sure you do it. Hug your cat and play with it, but also clean the litter box and make sure Fuzzy has food and water. You made the commitment, now follow through on it—like Noah did.

Dog—Man's Best Friend?

They say a dog is "man's best friend." Not a lot to look forward to, is it? You grow up, become a man, and your best friends will be dogs. Seriously though, dogs are friendly and loyal—and intelligent, if you don't count Dalmatians. These waggy-tailed wonders have been hanging out with people just about forever. Dogs watched over Job's sheep four thousand years ago (Job 30:1) and greyhounds—big skinny dogs, fast as lightning—were running around ancient Egypt.

The Egyptians even worshiped a dog god.

Maybe that's why after the Israelites left Egypt they didn't think too highly of dogs. Almost every time the Bible talks about dogs, well ... it's not too good. Sure, they had them, but these mangy Rovers were no pets. They hung out around cities, sticking their noses in garbage, eating dead bodies—including one queen—lapping blood off chariots, and licking the festering sores of beggars. Yum! (1 Kings 14:11; 22:38; 2 Kings 9:34–36; Luke 16:21).

If you think slurping garbage and blood is bad, the Bible also talks about sick puppies barfing up their stomach contents then going back and lapping up their own barf (2 Peter 2:22). You understand why the Israelites weren't crazy about dogs. And we haven't even mentioned how dogs lick their under parts or sometimes eat fresh cow poop—but since the Bible doesn't go there, we won't.

But after a while, dogs began to win people's hearts. Israelites in King David's day had dogs (Psalm 68:23). And they must have had watchdogs. Isaiah pointed out that some Israelites were like mute dogs, "they cannot bark; they lie around and dream, they love to sleep" (Isaiah 56:10–11). If you ever wondered if dogs dream, there you have it.

By New Testament times, dogs had wagged their tails all the way into the house and were eating under the table (Matthew 15:26–27).

Canines had become house pets. Mind you, the Greek word used here means little doggies, not 100-pound lobos.

Given half a chance, any dog, anywhere, any day of the week, will still do something grosser than you would care to watch, but these days people let it pass. "Mom! LOOK at what the dog's doing!" "Calm down, dear. Dogs don't know any better."

Egyptian God-Cats

The only cats mentioned in the Bible are lions and leopards. This doesn't mean house cats didn't exist in Bible days. They did. Big time. Egypt, right next door to Israel, was the cat capital of the planet. Modern cats are descended from African wild cats that the Egyptians tamed thousands of years ago.

There were scads of cats in Egypt. There had to be. Egypt was a major grain-producing country, and to protect all that grain they kept lots of cats and trained them to catch mice. Joseph was a practical guy, so when he piled up more grain than had ever been stored in all of Egypt's history (Genesis 41:47–49), you can be sure cats were a big part of his plan. He probably had armies of them!

Unfortunately, the Egyptians worshiped these mice-catching machines as gods and made statues of cat goddesses. It got so out of hand that if an Egyptian killed a cat, the punishment was usually death. When a pet cat died, people mourned by shaving off their eyebrows. Don't you do that! Deuteronomy 14:1 says, "Do not ... shave the front of your heads for the dead."

The Egyptians even embalmed dead cats. Whoo-OOO-eooww! Archaeologists have found a cat cemetery with more than 300,000 cat mummies in it. The way a lot of cats act today, you can see that they still want to be worshiped as gods. All this may be part of the reason the Israelites weren't into cats much after they left Egypt.

Pets in Heaven?

When your dog died, your grandmother probably patted you on the head and said, "Don't worry, you'll see him again in heaven." But maybe your big sister took you aside and said, "Animals don't have souls. When they're gone, they're gone." So who do you believe? What does the Bible say? Do animals go to heaven?

No one really knows. Even wise King Solomon admitted, "Who knows if the spirit of man rises upward and if the spirit of the animal goes down into the earth?"

However, even if Rover doesn't go to heaven,

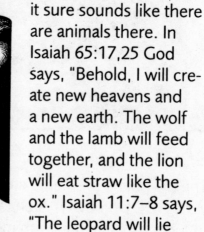

it sure sounds like there are animals there. In Isaiah 65:17,25 God says, "Behold, I will create new heavens and a new earth. The wolf and the lamb will feed together, and the lion will eat straw like the ox." Isaiah 11:7–8 says, "The leopard will lie down with the goat, the calf and the lion and the yearling together. The cow will feed with the bear... The infant will play near the hole of the cobra."

The most important thing is to make sure that *you're* going there. You don't want to miss out, do you? You might like resting your head on a great lion's shoulder. Or playing with vipers and cobras. Or riding on great white horses like the one Jesus will ride when he returns to earth.

Get COOLeR

Pets can be cool, especially if they're tarantulas or iguanas. But calling a dog "man's best friend"? Probably what that saying means is that a dog never gets mad at you and decides not to be your friend anymore. Once he's your friend, he's always your friend. But as Christians, we have a better friend than that. Jesus said that he would never leave us or stop acting like our friend. Also, we're supposed to be friends to our Christian friends like Jesus is to us, not fickle, worldly friends who decide to like you one day and then not talk to you the next. So enjoy pets, but remember they're third stringers as far as friends go.

ORDINARY KILLER ANIMALS

Lions

Lions no longer live in Israel—well, except in zoos—but they sure lived there in ancient times. Lions were symbols of courage, strength, and royalty. Solomon said lions were "mighty among beasts" and retreated before nothing (Proverbs 30:29–30). Jesus himself is called "the Lion of the tribe of Judah" (Revelation 5:5).

David wrote some psalms that sound like nature videos. Psalm 104:20–22 says, "It becomes night, and all the beasts of the forest prowl. The lions roar for their prey and seek their food from God. The sun rises, and they steal away; they return and lie down in their dens." Whoa!

Lions pray for prey? Well, lions are incredibly quiet when they sneak up on their food. Maybe they're saying one of those quiet prayers before their meal?

Some kings kept live lions chained to their thrones, but since this meant having to clean up lion poop, King Solomon had twelve carved lions on the steps of his throne—gold-covered, no less. Some kings kept lions in dens to eat up their enemies. Daniel was thrown into a den of lions, but God sent an angel to protect him, and he lived to tell the story (Daniel 6:16–24).

Then of course, there was the lion that tried to eat Samson. The strongman grabbed the lion and—RIIIIPPPP!—tore him apart. No one else living could've done that. Lions were the strongest and most ferocious feared felines in all Israel.

Leopards

Leopards used to live in Israel. "No way," you say? Way! King Solomon talked about "the mountain haunts of the leopards" (Song of Songs 4:8). Sometimes though, they waited outside cities to attack people (Jeremiah 5:6). These awesome animals were known for their ferocity and intelligence—and their beautiful, spotted coats. Jeremiah pointed out that just like some people can't change their ways, so a leopard can't change his spots (Jeremiah 13:23). But

God loves leopards. He promised that when the Messiah rules the earth, "the leopard will lie down with the goat," only this time the goat is not going to be inside the leopard (Isaiah 11:6).

Bears

Bears show up several times in the Bible, and the bear we are talking about here was not the polar bear, not the grizzly bear, but the Syrian brown bear. These bruisers mainly ate berries and stuff, but sometimes they ate meat, like the one that attacked David's sheep and was dropped by a well-aimed sling stone (1 Samuel 17:34–35).

Then there's Elisha and the bears: "Elisha went up to Bethel. As he was walking along the road, some youths came out of the town and jeered at him. 'Go on up, you baldhead!' they said. 'Go on up, you baldhead!' He turned around, looked at them, and called down a curse on them in the name of the Lord. Then two bears came out of the woods and mauled forty-two of the youths" (2 Kings 2:23–24).

These young punks were ungodly boys who were not serving God and were basically saying that Elisha and his God were powerless. What happened to them was a picture of what God was trying to get across to his people. If you continue to rebel, you'll be destroyed. It really had nothing to do with calling someone "baldy." But if that were the punishment for name-calling, there would be a lot of bear attacks!

Wolves

In ancient Israel, packs of wolves used to hide out in the woods. These smart creatures are very cool, loyal, and brave. Only problem is, they lived in the middle of sheep coun-try and sheep were just so delicious, so slow, and so dumb that wolves couldn't resist eating them. That made wolves the enemy of shepherds, who were constantly defending their slow, dumb, delicious sheep.

The Bible talks a lot about wolves. It says they attack in the evenings, scattering sheep flocks and tearing their prey apart. Oh yeah, and they're messy eaters. It also points out that wolf packs are fair in divvying up the night's kill (John 10:12; Genesis 49:27). In John 10:1–16, Jesus said that Christians were like sheep and he was the Good Shepherd, protecting us from wolves—who, in this case, symbolize the forces of evil. Jesus wasn't saying that we are slow and dumb, but that we can rely on him to guide us and keep us from evil as we stay close to him.

Jackals

Jackals are wild dogs that look kind of like foxes. Arabs call them "howlers" because of their mournful cry. Jackals often eat dead animals—in fact, in many countries, they're like street cleaners. Of course, jackals mostly live in the wilderness. They're not thought of as very noble animals—sort of like vultures without wings. When Job wanted to complain how low he had sunk, he moaned, "I have become a brother of jackals" (Job 30:29).

Hyenas

Striped hyenas were common in ancient Israel. Ever see nature shows where hyenas are gathered around something dead at night, ripping out big chunkos of meat; their eyeballs are glowing and they're laughing hideously? Bible guys knew about hyenas. Isaiah prophesied that after God destroyed Babylon, "hyenas will howl in her strongholds" (Isaiah 13:22). You know God had a sense of humor when he created hyenas. They have a weird howl that sounds like a hysterical human laugh. So who got the last laugh?

Foxes

The Bible talks about foxes nine times, and each time it's talking about the common fox of Palestine, *Vulpes vulgaris*. (That's fox, by the way, not vulgar Vulcan.) Foxes first appear in the Bible in Judges 15:3–5, when Samson caught 300 of them, tied burning torches to their tails, and set them loose in the Philistine's wheat fields. Wonder how he managed to catch all those foxes when even one fox can sometimes outfox a hundred hunters and hounds!

The saying "outfox" came from the fact that foxes are known for being very smart and tricky. When Jesus called King Herod a fox (Luke 13:32), Jesus wasn't saying that he had a pointy face, he was pointing out that Herod was crafty like a fox.

Weasels

The only thing the Bible says about weasels is that you shouldn't eat them (Leviticus 11:29)— if you're Jewish, that is. If you're a Gentile and you're really hungry, go for it. Weasel in a bun? Footlong weasel? Weasel on a stick? Hey, it could catch on! Just put on plenty of relish.

Maulings and Manglings

In Bible days when cities became ruins, they filled up with jackals, hyenas, goats, owls, and falcons (Isaiah 34:11–15). Bad enough. But when people emptied out of an entire country, wild animals moved in big time! This happened when the Israelites were taken captive to Assyria. Some pagans moved in, saw all the orchards and vineyards and thought, *Sweeet! All these goodies up for grabs.* Only problem was, the lions were looking at the pagans and thinking the same thing (2 Kings 17:24–25).

In Jeremiah's day, the Judeans had forsaken
God to worship idols and were so cruel and
selfish, that it was like God opened all the
cage doors at the zoo to teach them that if
they were going to act like animals, then they
were fair game. Lions attacked them in the for-
ests, wolves ravaged them in the deserts, and
leopards shredded anyone who came out the
city gates (Jeremiah 5:6). Whew!

GET SMARTER

The Bible says that the Devil is like a roaring lion looking for someone to devour. Yikes! How does he pick who's for his snack? Well, just like a lion, he probably chooses someone who looks weak or is away from the rest of the herd. The Devil uses lies to try draw Christians into sin and away from other Christians. Peter said that we should be self-controlled, resist the Devil, and stand firm in the faith. If we don't yield to the lies, we'll be like Daniel—he was in the lion's den all night, but he was untouched. James said that if you resist the Devil he will flee from you!

Ravenous Reptiles

Snakes

Snakes are cool! Ever think, "Man, I like snakes" and then your sister says, "Snakes are a symbol of ee-vill." That was true of the snake in the garden of Eden, but you can't give all snakes a bad rep for that. Wise King Solomon admired snakes! He said, "Here are three things that are too amazing for me," then he listed number two as "the way of a snake on a rock" (Proverbs 30:18–19). So tell your sister that snakes rock!

The next time you see a dude with a big old boa slung over his neck and you go, "Cool!" and your sister screams, "Yecchh! That is soooo sick!"—tell her, "Hey! When God sets up his kingdom on earth, he's gonna let toddlers play with cobras and vipers" (Isaiah 11:8). The only reason they can't play with them now is because those suckers are poisonous. Hmmmm. Since boas aren't poisonous, can you play with them

now? (Not a good idea! They can kill you by crushing you in their coils.)

Think about this: When God wanted to show the Israelites that Moses had divine authority, what did he give him? A walking stick that doubled as a snake (Exodus 3:3–4). This snake was probably the Egyptian cobra, a most princely serpent that grows to be 8 ½ feet long! ("Hey Mom! Moses carried a snake around! Can I have one?" "Ummm ... ask your father.")

One last cool snake fact, then we're done: in Numbers 21:4–9, when the Israelites murmured about the manna, God sent poisonous snakes to bite them. When they wailed for mercy, Moses made a bronze serpent and put it up on a pole. Anyone who looked at snakey was healed. And guess what? Jesus compared himself to that serpent (John 3:14–15). Jesus was put on a cross and died for our sins, and when we look to him, our sins are forgiven. So are serpents always a symbol of evil? No way, dude! Tell that to your sister!

Lizards and Reptiles

Chameleons are incredible lizards that change color to blend in with different-color backgrounds. The chameleon of ancient Israel lived in wooded areas. If you were a chameleon, your favorite Bible verse would be Leviticus 11:30, which forbade the Jews to eat chameleons. Yeah! One less predator to have to change color for.

Will you geckos stop falling? In America free-falling geckos are not a big problem, but in many countries they scamper across the walls and ceilings, burping and chirping, then Whoops! their little suction feet lose their suck and down they plop into your bed or porridge or hair. This was such a big problem in Israel, that Moses spent ten verses talking about how to deal with it (Leviticus 11:29–38).

The Bible also talks about the great lizard, the monitor lizard, the wall lizard, and the skink (Leviticus 11:30). That's skinks—not skunks. There are some 600 different species of skinks in the world, and they all have scaly tongues and long bodies. The skink mentioned in the Bible is the common skink, also called *Scincus scincus*. Impress the guy behind the counter next time you go into the pet shop. Ask, "Would you by chance happen to have a *Scincus scincus* for sale?"

The crocodile isn't mentioned by name, but the Hebrews in Egypt knew all about these gargantuan green reptiles. They should've! Crocs crawled in the canals a few feet from their doorsteps. When Pharaoh ordered, "Every boy that is born you must throw into the Nile" (Exodus 1:22), he was talking about throwing the Hebrew boys to the crocs! Where's the guy who wrestles crocs when you need him?

Frogs

The scientific name for frogs is *Ranidae*. When gazillions of frogs hopped out of the streams and canals of the Nile and the Ranidae overran Egypt, God was sending them as a judgment. The frogs devastated Egypt (Psalm 78:45). You gotta wonder if the frogs took this chance to get revenge on all the Egyptian boys who had caught and tormented them. Payback time! Ha ha! Whoooo-heeeee! Lookit 'em run!

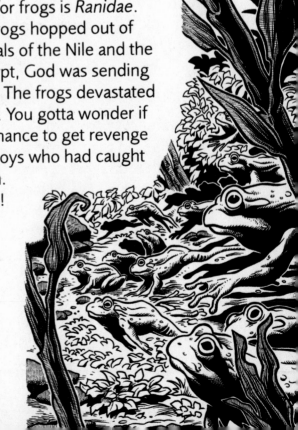

Ramesses had been a kid once. Now frogs came into his palace, his bedroom, and his bed (Exodus 8:1–6). "Hi Ramesses!

Remember us? We're the Ranidae and weeeee're baaaaaack!"

It was miracle enough to make zillions of frogs swarm out of the Nile; the backup miracle was that when Moses prayed, all those frogs began dropping dead the next day. They just all croaked. They died in homes, courtyards, and fields. "They were piled into heaps, and the land reeked" (Exodus 8:8–14). Phew-eee!

Ever heard the expression, "Got a frog in your throat?" Well, in Revelation 16:13, evil spirits that looked like frogs came out of the mouth of the Antichrist and the False Prophet. You got to hate evil spirits, and the Antichrist guy is trouble—but Ranidae rule! (A few at a time, though!)

Dinosaurs Rule!—Or Used To

Dinosaurs are some of the absolutely coolest animals God ever made. There is really nothing on earth today that compares with them. After watching some of Hollywood's dinosaur movies, you may wonder, "Man! Why did all those mega-monsters have to become extinct? They're so utterly awesome." But as a scientist in one of those movies pointed out, "First it's all 'Oooh! Ahhh!' That's how it always starts. Then later there's running and screaming." Imagine what a different world we would be living in if dinosaurs were still here! So why did they become extinct?

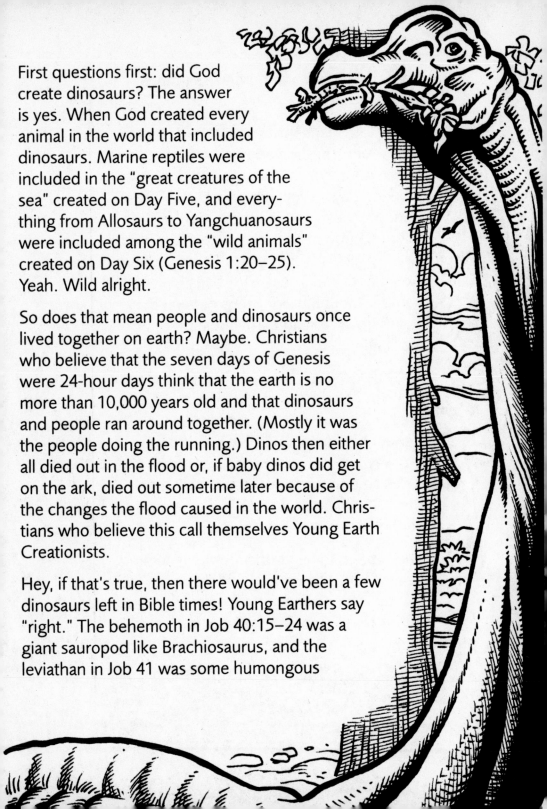

First questions first: did God create dinosaurs? The answer is yes. When God created every animal in the world that included dinosaurs. Marine reptiles were included in the "great creatures of the sea" created on Day Five, and everything from Allosaurs to Yangchuanosaurs were included among the "wild animals" created on Day Six (Genesis 1:20–25). Yeah. Wild alright.

So does that mean people and dinosaurs once lived together on earth? Maybe. Christians who believe that the seven days of Genesis were 24-hour days think that the earth is no more than 10,000 years old and that dinosaurs and people ran around together. (Mostly it was the people doing the running.) Dinos then either all died out in the flood or, if baby dinos did get on the ark, died out sometime later because of the changes the flood caused in the world. Christians who believe this call themselves Young Earth Creationists.

Hey, if that's true, then there would've been a few dinosaurs left in Bible times! Young Earthers say "right." The behemoth in Job 40:15–24 was a giant sauropod like Brachiosaurus, and the leviathan in Job 41 was some humongous

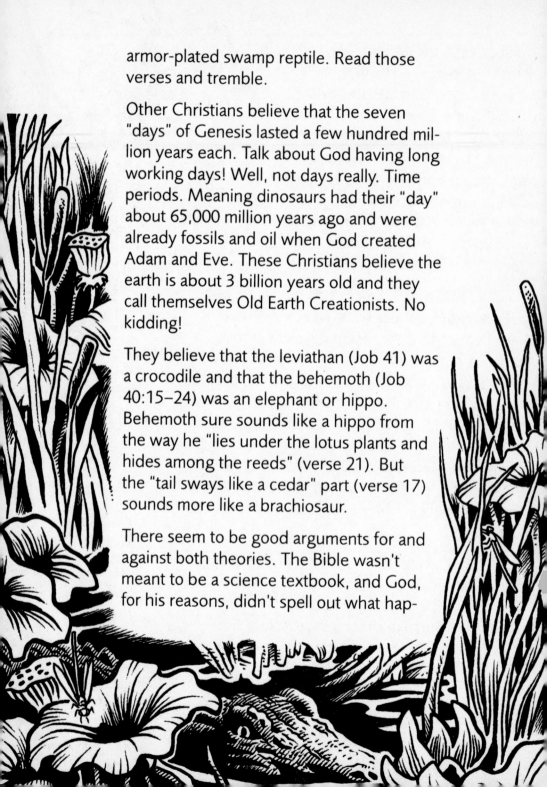

armor-plated swamp reptile. Read those verses and tremble.

Other Christians believe that the seven "days" of Genesis lasted a few hundred million years each. Talk about God having long working days! Well, not days really. Time periods. Meaning dinosaurs had their "day" about 65,000 million years ago and were already fossils and oil when God created Adam and Eve. These Christians believe the earth is about 3 billion years old and they call themselves Old Earth Creationists. No kidding!

They believe that the leviathan (Job 41) was a crocodile and that the behemoth (Job 40:15–24) was an elephant or hippo. Behemoth sure sounds like a hippo from the way he "lies under the lotus plants and hides among the reeds" (verse 21). But the "tail sways like a cedar" part (verse 17) sounds more like a brachiosaur.

There seem to be good arguments for and against both theories. The Bible wasn't meant to be a science textbook, and God, for his reasons, didn't spell out what happened to dinosaurs. So hippo or brachio? Or is it a third option altogether? Your guess is as good as any. Either way, remember, God created dinosaurs. Hey, wouldn't that be cool if there was a huge zoo in heaven that had all the creatures that God ever created—including dinos? Wow!

Get Deeper

The most famous reptile story in the Bible involved an infamous serpent. Picture this: Adam and Eve are living in Paradise with God—no sadness, everything happy and perfect. But the Devil somehow convinces Eve that she'd be better off doing things another way. He's the greatest con artist ever—Jesus called him the Father of Lies! And he's still at it. We're busy serving God and he tries to tell us we'd be better off doing things our own way, or not listening to God, or that we'd have a better life in the world. He's the grandaddy of all liars and cons. He's been using the same con for thousands of years and people still fall for it. The truth is, following God, who loves us and wants the best for us, is going back to Paradise.

Dodos and Ostriches

Dodos were flightless birds. They just stood there (duh) while men went around beaning them on the heads with clubs. Bonk, bonk, bonk. One too many bonks and soon all the dodos were extinct. That's why clueless people are called dodos. Ostriches are dumb too. Job 39:17 says that God did not give ostriches a share of good sense. Dodos' stupidity sent them to extinction-land, but ostriches are still here. Why? Being fast makes up for lack of

brains. Job 39:13–18 says, "When she spreads her feathers to run, she laughs at horse and rider." Hoooo-hoo-hoo! Lookit me! I'm fast as liiiiiiightning! I may be stupid but heee-yuk, lookit me run!" (Ostriches can peel out at 40 mph.) So remember the difference between the dodo and the ostrich next time someone wants to club you!

Swallows

Ever see birds darting overhead, feasting on insects? Swallows can spend hours in the air without landing. Proverbs 26:2 describes "a darting swallow" that "does not come to rest." No wonder they're called swallows. Gulp! Gulp! Okay, to the left! Gulp! Gulp! To the right! Gulp. (Like playing the VeggieTales® Space Corn computer game all afternoon.)

Ever hear of holy swallows? That's not drinking grape juice at communion. One of Korah's kids noticed that some swallows had built nests inside the temple near the altar (Psalm 84:3). The Israelites went to the temple to worship, but these birds lived there! The priests were so impressed that the swallows chose to live near the altar that they left their nests there. They probably had doctrinal arguments about it for months though.

Sparrows

Sparrows were so common in Israel that they almost didn't count. They were so cheap that if you bought four you'd get a fifth one thrown in for free (Matthew 10:29,31; Luke 12:6). Yet Jesus said that not even one sparrow was forgotten by God. The moral?

You are worth more than many sparrows. God knows everything you're going through and he cares. So don't be afraid—talk to him and trust him. Wow, that's a big lesson from a sparrow!

Eagles

The eagle mentioned in the Bible is probably the crowned eagle, the largest eagle in Africa. God described how eagles lived: Job 39:27–30 says, "He dwells on a cliff... From there he seeks out his food; his eyes detect it from afar. His young ones feast on blood, and where the slain are, there is he." Feast on blood? Yum! If that doesn't make you want to be an eagle, nothing will.

The Bible describes eagles as having "powerful wings" (Ezekiel 17:3,7), but they're so big and heavy they can't make sharp turns to chase their prey around. That's why eagles swoop down in surprise attacks instead.

The eagle is a symbol of power and majesty. In fact, God described himself as an eagle and Israel as eagle chicks. Moses said, "he guarded him ... like an eagle that stirs up its nest and hovers over its young, and spreads its wings to catch them and carries them on its pinions" (Deuteronomy 32:10–11).

Cool! We're like eagles too when we trust him. God promises that "those who hope in the Lord will renew their strength. They will soar on wings like eagles" (Isaiah 40:31). Gone soaring with the eagles today, or are you running with turkeys?

Owls

Owls are just too cool! These eerie, unblinking night hunters are mentioned over and over again in the Bible. Leviticus 11:13–18 talks about eight kinds of owls: the eagle owl, short- and long-eared owls, wood owl, fisher owl, screech owl, little owl, and scops owl. Owls lived in the deserts, ruined cities, and holes in the rocks.

When Job said that he had become "a companion of owls" (Job 30:29), he wasn't saying he went flying, hunting mice at night when the moon was full; he meant that he felt lonely and forsaken. King David also said, "I am like a desert owl" (Psalm 102:6).

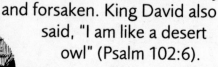

He wasn't hunting for mice either.

And hey, owls are grateful too. God said they would honor him because he provided water in the wilderness (Isaiah 43:20). So owls may be lonely, but you can't say that they don't give a hoot!

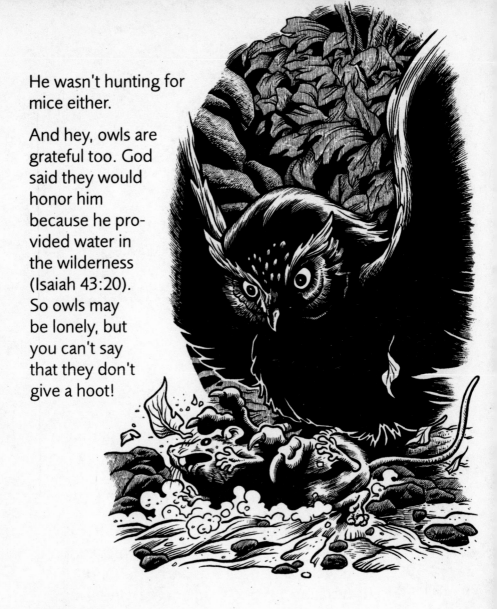

Vultures

When the Bible talks about vultures, it's talking about the *Aegypius monachus*, a vulture with a wingspan of nine feet that weighs in at twenty-seven pounds. Wow! Lie down for a nap in the desert and—Thump! Thump!

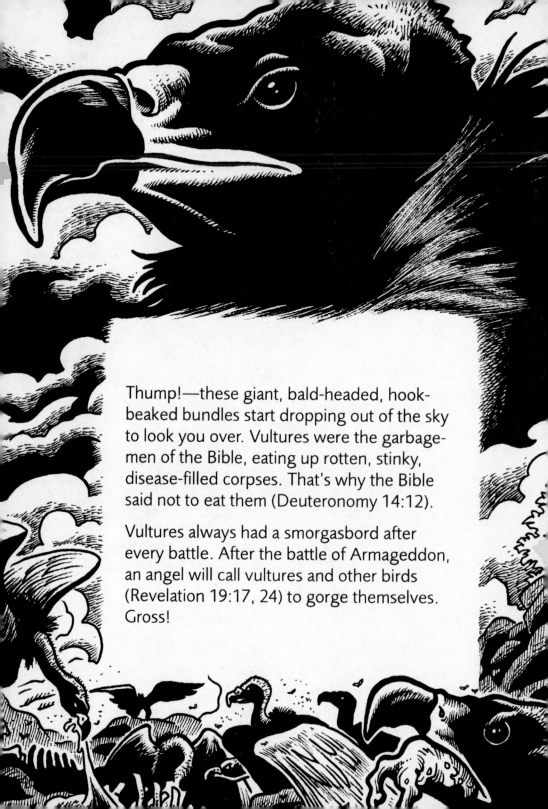

Thump!—these giant, bald-headed, hook-beaked bundles start dropping out of the sky to look you over. Vultures were the garbage-men of the Bible, eating up rotten, stinky, disease-filled corpses. That's why the Bible said not to eat them (Deuteronomy 14:12).

Vultures always had a smorgasbord after every battle. After the battle of Armageddon, an angel will call vultures and other birds (Revelation 19:17, 24) to gorge themselves. Gross!

Get Smarter

Ostriches are fast, eagles are strong and have great eyesight, swallows have great stamina, and owls can hunt at night. They all have strengths that match the job and life that God gave them. God gave us all different talents and strengths. We can't all be good at everything. But God has given us all a unique set of gifts and talents that match what he has planned for us and what he knows our lives hold in store. So develop your gifts, seek his plan for your life, and follow him daily. You'll be amazed at how the way God made you matches what he gives you to do.

CREEPY, CRAWLY CRITTERS

Locusts and Locust Plagues

Locusts are like grasshoppers, only bigger and hungrier. They often come together in great swarms of millions of locusts, and migrate hundreds of miles. The sky turns black when they fly over, and wherever they land they eat everything green.

Because Pharaoh refused to free the Hebrew slaves, God sent a hailstorm on Egypt that "beat down everything growing in the fields and stripped every tree" (Exodus 9:25). Then God sent a giant locust swarm. "They devoured all that was left after the hail ... Nothing green remained" (Exodus 10:4, 15). One good thing: they cleaned up all the flattened crops and rub-

bish. Cleanup? Who needs a rake? Here come the locusts! "Hey Dad, let's get a pet locust swarm and we won't have to rake the leaves." Not!

There was this guy named Joel, and in his day the biggest locust plague that had ever happened hit Israel. God sent in five—count 'em, five!—waves of locust armies, one after another, to eat up everything in sight (Joel 1:4). Joel said, "Before them the land is like the garden of Eden, behind them, a desert waste" (Joel 2:3). This was like Insect Armageddon. Imagine huddling inside your house hearing the roar of millions of locust wings.

Locust plagues didn't just happen in Bible days: they still happen today—mostly in Africa—and there's still nothing you can do except hide in your house till they eat all the greenery in sight, then leave. "They come, they eat, they leave!"

Filthy Flies

Ever go bananas trying to kill a fly? In Exodus 8:24 "dense swarms of flies poured into Pharaoh's palace and into the houses of his officials, and throughout Egypt the land was ruined by the flies." Ruined, all right! Flies crawl around in dung, gobs of it stick to their hairy legs, then drop every- where the flies walk—on your food, on your bed, on your clothes, on you.

In the New Testament the Devil is called Beelzebub, "the lord of the flies" (Mark 3:22). When you picture flies swarming around a manure pile, that's a picture of the Devil's king- dom.

Wanna learn something really cool? Usually when worms are mentioned in the Bible, these are not earthworms or fishing worms. Nuh uh. These are little white fly larvae: maggots!—the kind that breed in your garbage when you miss garbage pickup.

The Bible talks a lot about maggots eating corpses. Job 21:26 says that when people die "they lie in the dust, and worms cover them." This is not cover them like a blanket to keep them warm. Shall we make it clearer? Job 24:20 says that "the worm feasts on them."

Job 25:5–6 says that men are "but maggots" and the sons of men are "only worms." Maggot? Worm? Take your pick. The point is humans without God don't amount to much. Fortunately, Jesus died for us so that we can be God's children. And God doesn't have maggots for kids. Those are the children of the "lord of the flies."

Of Moths and Men

The moth mentioned in the Bible is usually the clothes moth. God likes to use the moth to teach us that this life and the things in it are fragile and not as important as we may think. Jesus taught that we shouldn't store up treasures, here on earth where rust corrodes and the moth eats them.

Job said, "The house he builds is like a moth's cocoon." It's fragile and soon gone (Job 27:18). Not just his house is gone, but the guy too! He is "crushed more readily than a moth" (Job 4:19). Ever accidentally wipe out a moth? Well, in God's eyes, that's how weak and short-lived people are in this physical world.

God isn't against moths or life or things in it. He just wants us to know that loving him, loving others, and the life to come are what is important. Chewing clothes seems like a small job, but the lesson God gave the moth to teach is a big one.

Scorpions

Scorpions are arachnids, and these nasty creatures are often found in deserts. They have large pincers and a curving stinger tail. God led the Israelites through the Sinai desert where they met—and were probably stung by—lots and lots of scorpions (Deuteronomy 8:15).

King Solomon was super wise, but his son Rehoboam missed out in the brains department. In his first royal speech he promised the Israelites that if they let him be their king, he would whip and scourge them with scorpions. Wow! Who wrote that speech for him? Two-thirds of Israel didn't want to be tortured and left this new scorpion

king (1 Kings 12:11–17). Surprise, surprise!

Now imagine dragging yourself to the breakfast table and your dad asks what you want. You mumble, "Scrambled eggs." A few minutes later he scrapes a scorpion from the frying pan into your plate. "Watch out for the tail," he says. "Eat that and it'll kill you. The rest of it tastes like cockroach." Unless your dad is truly weird, this little scene will never happen. God is good, and Jesus said that just as dads wouldn't give scorpions to their sons, if you ask God for good things he won't give you bad stuff (Luke 11:11–12).

When Jesus said that he gave his followers authority to trample on scorpions (Luke 10:18–20), he was talking about power over evil spirits, not actual scorpions. Just thought we'd mention that in case you wanted to test this verse out on your next visit to the desert. Or, of course, if your dad tries the scorpion and eggs thing.

Slugs and Salt

King David complained about his enemies, then said, "Let them vanish like ... a slug melting away as it moves along" (Psalm 58:7–8). This isn't sluggo leaving a trail of slime. Apparently David had spilled some salt on a slug and noticed how the little guy dissolved—like the Wicked Witch of the West when Dorothy doused her with water. David wished he could get rid of his enemies so easily.

It's funny that Jesus said that we are the salt of the earth (Matthew 5:13). That's our New Testament weapon against the wicked—leading them away from the world and toward Christ by loving them and living godly lives.

Spiders and Spider Webs

The Bible doesn't say much about spiders. It seems like everyone would like to not mention them or have them around. But it does teach two life lessons using the spider's web. Isaiah 59:5 says that the wicked "spin a spider's web"

but that "their cobwebs are useless for clothing; they cannot cover themselves with what they make." Well, noooo. Can you imagine running around dressed in nothing but spider webs? We are not talking Spider-Man here—more like streaking! In other words, wickedness gets you nothing and nowhere fast.

Imagine walking with a friend through the woods. You're hot and exhausted. You stop to lean against a tree but your 200-pound friend spies a spider's web, leans on it, falls right through—Of course! What did he expect?—and tumbles down a ravine. Job 8:13–15 teaches that trusting in things instead of God is like leaning on a spider's web.

Ants Without Rulers Rule!

Ever watch a busy anthill and see them little guys just go, go, go all over, running this way and that, carrying grain, grass, and dead bugs? In Proverbs 6:6; 30; 24–25 Solomon says that the ant is "extremely wise." Why? "It has no commander, no overseer or ruler, yet it stores its provisions in summer and gathers its food at harvest." No dad reminding it to go to the store. No mom begging it to

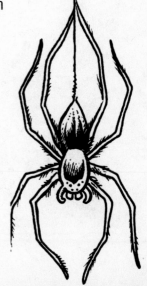

set the table. It just does it. Now that's smart! Okay, extremely wise.

The type of ant Solomon described here is the harvester ant. They live in areas of the world where there's not much food, so they store up seeds for lean times. Harvester ants are so good at what they do that they live on every continent except Antarctica. They divide up the labor and then everyone just does their job. Go, ants, go!

Get Stronger

Don't bug me! Actually, let's rethink that. Nothing can stop a swarm of locust all working together like one giant uni-mind bug. Harvester ants all work hard and they succeed almost everywhere around the world. One thing we all hate is bugs as a mass or in swarms—it's the stuff scary movies are made of. Why? Because a single little bug is easy to squish, but huge numbers of them working together can do what they want—and can't be squished. That's how God wants us to think in the church, the body of Christ. No matter what country we were born in, what the color of our skin is, or what church we go to, if we all love and accept each other and work together, all doing our part, the church of Jesus Christ will be strong on the earth. No squish! (Ephesians 4:16.)

The Amazing Bible Diet

Those of you who like roasted rats on a stick (some people do!) will be disappointed to learn that they were on the do-not-eat list for Israelites (Leviticus 11:29). That didn't stop some Israelites from enjoying them anyway (Isaiah 66:17). "Hey honey! Throw some extra rats in the soup! We have visitors."

Insects were another matter: "You may eat any kind of locust, katydid, cricket or grasshopper. But all other winged creatures that have four legs you are to detest" (Leviticus 11:22). Good point. Next time you go to eat a winged bug, count its legs first.

If you think people on TV talk about strange diets (nothing but grapefruit and carrot juice), remember, all John the Baptist ate, day after day, was locusts and wild honey (Matthew 3:4). All Elijah ate for three and a half years was bread, and at first he was on the raven-served diet (1 Kings 17:1–6; 15–16). For forty years the Israelites were on the angel food diet: almost all they ate was manna (Numbers 11:4–6). And Jesus was on the air diet for forty days while fasting (Matthew 4:1–2).

In the Old Testament, God gave a long, detailed list of the kinds of animals the Israelites couldn't eat, but in Acts 10:9–15, God gave Peter a vision of all kinds of four-footed animals, as well as reptiles of the earth and birds of the air that were all on the don't-eat list. Then a voice told him, "Get up Peter. Kill and eat." God actually used this vision to show Peter that the Jews needed to begin telling everyone that Jesus died for them, not just Jews. See, the Jews had thought that non-Jews were unclean just like inedible food. Now God wanted the Jews to start thinking of the Gentiles as potential believers. The New Testament also went on to teach that Christians didn't have to follow the Old Testament lists of things to eat and not eat. Oh wow! So now you can eat monitor lizards, skunks, vultures, and centipedes? "Um, surrrrre. Thanks for the option but you guys go ahead. I'm really not hungry."

MISCELLANEOUS BIBLE BEASTS

Solomon Goes Ape

King Solomon had a fleet of trading ships that went down the coast of Africa and brought back apes (probably gorillas) and baboons (1 Kings 10:22). Baboons are short-tailed monkeys that sort of look like dogs. You can see Solomon chaining a couple gorillas to his throne to impress visiting kings ("Wow! You got a gorilla? I gotta get me one!"), but you really gotta wonder why he'd want to fill up his palace with baboons. Can't you just see them grooming people, looking for lice? Besides, baboons bite! Maybe he had a zoo.

Rodents in the Rocks

Know what coneys are? No, they're not extra-small ice cream cones. Coneys are rock badgers—furry little critters as big as rabbits. The Bible says, "Coneys are creatures of little power, yet they make their home in the crags" (Proverbs 30:26). Smart! If you don't have muscles, protect yourself by using your brains. See ya in the rock pile?

Hunting Antelope

The Israelites used to hunt gazelles (Isaiah 13:14). Often they threw nets over them (Isaiah 51:20). Since gazelles could run 50 mph, however, it's not like people ran behind them with nets. 2 Samuel 2:18 says Ashael "was as fleet-footed as a wild gazelle" but you gotta know that Ashy wasn't clocking 50 mph. So how did they net gazelles? They waited for them at water holes. That's an old lion trick, by the way.

When Bears Become Stars

Some bears are stars, and we don't mean Country Bears. When Job said God was "the Maker of the Bear" (Job 9:9), or when God asked Job, "Can you ... lead out the Bear with its cubs?" they were talking about a constellation of stars.

Animals in a Rainstorm

Ever see your dog huddle in his doghouse during a rainstorm? You call him, "C'mon boy! C'mon!" but he doesn't come? Duh! Job's pal Elihu spent six verses describing a wild rainstorm—complete with sky-splitting lightning and roaring thunder—then said, "The animals take cover; they remain in their dens" (Job 37:1–8). Well, yeaaah. Lots of people get killed by lightning every year. This is an obvious thing we can learn from animals: take cover during storms.

Baa, Moo, and Oink

Sheep

Sheep were the first domestic (tamed) animals mentioned in the Bible. Adam and Eve's son Abel raised sheep. When it came time to make an offering to the Lord, he sacrificed the first-born lamb (Genesis 4:2–4). Ever since then, Bible people have sacrificed sheep as offerings to God. In fact, sheep are mentioned more times in the Bible than any other animal. The Israelites enjoyed eating mutton (sheep meat) even though they mostly raised sheep for their wool and milk. Yeah, you read that right: sheep milk. Famous Bible heros like Abraham, Moses, and David were shepherds.

Sheep were easy to raise in Israel's dry climate. Another thing is, sheep are very peaceful and docile. *Docile* means "easy to manage." That's why your mom sometimes wishes you were more sheep-like. Being all wooly-white and sweet and docile made sheep a symbol of innocence and purity. Jesus himself was called "the Lamb of God ... a lamb without blemish or defect" (John 1:29; 1 Peter 1:19).

Goats

Ever since the earliest days, nomadic herdsmen kept flocks of goats (Genesis 4:2; 27:9; 30:32). Yet Jesus tells one parable where sheep symbolize the righteous and goats the wicked (Matthew 25:31–34, 41) and some folks go overboard and think goats are evil. No way. The Bible goes on and on how great goats are. The Israelites offered goats as sacrifices to God, they made God's holy tent out of goat hair, drank goat's milk, and used goat's skins as water jugs. (Imagine taking that kind of water jug to a baseball game!) Goats are cool!

Cattle

Modern cattle are descended from the wild ox, the aurochs. The first cowboy mentioned in the Bible was Jabal. "He was the father of those who live in tents and raise livestock" (Genesis 4:19). Jabal probably didn't ride horses but he was a nomadic herdsman, leading his cattle on the wide open range. Yippie-kay-yo-kai-yay!

After the Israelites defeated the Midianites in battle, there was one very huge dust cloud as the battle-boys bopped on home. Why? Along with all the other spoils of war they were driving a herd of 72,000 cattle (Numbers 31:33). The Midianites probably thought this was the biggest cattle rustling heist in history.

Since cattle need good pasture, the Israelites had fewer cows and more sheep and goats. Their best cattle country was in places like Gilead and Bashan. That's why the tribes of Reuben and Gad, who had large herds of cattle, wanted to live there (Numbers 32:1–5). Later on, Bashan became famous for its bulls (Psalm 22:12). Probably for its steaks too! "Bashan Steak House, here we come!"

Porky Pigs

The pig was considered a filthy animal (Leviticus 11:7), so though it was easy to raise, the Israelites didn't keep herds of pigs or eat their meat.

There were wild pigs in Israel, and people built stone walls around their vineyards to keep out robbers and pigs. God said his people were like a vineyard full of ripe grapes, but because they'd sinned, "boars from the forest ravaged it" (Psalm 80:8–13). We are talking about pigs piggin' out!

You can tell what the Israelites thought about pigs by the things they used them to teach. Solomon compared a woman who looked good on the outside but not on the inside to a pig with a gold ring in its nose (Proverbs 11:22). Peter said a backslider was like a washed sow returning to—Kerr-Splaaaat!—wallow in the muck (2 Peter 2:22). Jesus said not to throw pearls of wisdom to pigs or they'll just trample them in the mud, then turn around and attack you (Matthew 7:6). In other words, don't try to

give the truth to people who don't want it.

Once when a Greek king wanted to freak out the Jews, he sacrificed a pig on the temple altar. The Jews freaked all right. They started a war and kicked the Greeks' butts right out of Israel. They then took out the old altar, built a new one, and rededicated the temple to God. Every year after that they celebrated the Feast of Dedication. Jesus celebrated one of those feasts (John 10:22–23).

In Jesus' day, thousands of Greeks and Romans lived in Israel, and they raised pigs. Jesus once sent demons into a herd of their pigs. The pigs promptly leaped off a cliff and drowned (Mark 5:11–13). Today lots of people like pigs for the chops, ham, sausage, and bacon, but still don't think very highly of them. It's still not nice to compare someone to a pig. Then there's Miss Piggy.

BEASTS OF BURDEN

Horses

A lot of girls have this thing about horses: "Ohhhh, they're such lovely, peaceful creatures." Yeah, but from the first time horses are mentioned in the Bible to the last time they gallop across its pages, they are mostly warhorses, snorting and striking terror into the enemy as they race into battle—not cute little prancing show horses.

Listen to this description of a warhorse from the book of Job: "He paws fiercely, rejoicing in his strength, and charges into the fray ... In frenzied excitement he eats up the ground; he cannot

stand still when the trumpet sounds ... He catches the scent of battle from afar" (Job 39:19–25).

"Frenzied excitement?" Cool. And here's the apostle John's vision: "I saw heaven standing open and there before me was a white horse, whose rider is called Faithful and True. With justice he judges and makes war. The armies of heaven were following him, riding on white horses" (Revelation 19:11–15). Can you imagine Jesus returning to earth leading an army all on white warhorses?

Funny thing is, between Job and John, people in that area of the world didn't ride horses into war—they used them to pull chariots. And in Israel, chariots weren't the big thing. Therefore horses weren't really the cool animal to have. Donkeys? Sure. Camels? Bring 'em on. Oxcarts? Yup! Horses? Well, no.

Egypt had horses and chariots (Exodus 14:9), but not the Israelites. Not until King David's day.

When King David fought the king of Zobah, he captured 1,000 chariot horses (2 Samuel 8:3–4). David was awed by horses. He recognized they were the ultimate battle weapons. That's why he reminded the Israelites to trust in God rather than horses (Psalm 20:7). Sure, he admitted, horses were awesome, but when it came down to it, "despite all its great strength it cannot save" (Psalm 33:17). Meaning that horses are utterly cool, powerful, fast, magnificent animals, but don't think you'll win a battle because you have a horse, but because you trust God.

The Israelites soon became horse-lovers and all their kings went rippin' around Israel in horse-drawn chariots. Solomon even became a horse-trader (1 Kings 10:28–29). "Solomon had four thousand stalls for chariot horses and twelve thousand horses" (1 Kings 4:26). Sol put it this way: "The horse is made ready for the day of battle, but victory rests with the Lord" (Proverbs 21:31).

Well, if Job, David, and Solomon think horses are cool, and Jesus will be riding one out of heaven, they've gotta be great. The snorting, frenzied war-horses, that is, not the pretty kind with pink ribbons in their manes.

Donkeys and Wild Donkeys

Before horses came along, the Israelites used donkeys to carry people, lug loads, pull carts, and drag plows. Donkeys are small and bumpy to ride, but they're sure-footed, which counts a lot in rugged terrain like Israel. Even princes and kings rode on donkeys. Balaam rode a donkey all the way from the Euphrates to Moab. Jesus himself rode a donkey into Jerusalem (Judges 12:13–14; Numbers 22:4–5, 21; Matthew 21:1–7).

The wild donkey, on the other hand, didn't have

to pull carts or obey orders. He got to run free in the wastelands and salt flats. Hey! All the salt you can lick! (Salt flats are also where they test- drive cars at 300 mph, which has got to be hard on the wild donkey pop-ulation.)

God said that Esau would be "a wild donkey of a man" (Genesis 16:12). That doesn't mean he turned into a donkey like Pinocchio did. It just meant he was wild and liked open spaces—and was noisy. (Job 6:5 talks about the noise wild donkeys make when they're hungry.) Here's another wild don-key proverb: Zophar said, "A witless man can no more become wise than a wild donkey's colt can be born a man" (Job 11:12). You see, it works both ways: people can't turn into donkeys and donkeys can't turn into people.

Camels

Camels! Ah, can't live with them, can't live without them. These magnificent, gangly-legged, wobbly humped, curvy-necked, big-lipped beasts are so useful for carrying heavy loads that they're called the "ships of the desert." When they start spitting and biting, they're called other names as well! Yet from ancient times till today, desert nomads can't do without them.

Abraham had plenty of camels, and Job had 3,000 of them (Genesis 12:16; Job 1:3). Before horses became popular, people rode camels into war. It was a bit of a wobbly ride, rocking back and forth as you charged. The Midianites rode war camels and loved their mounts so much they hung golden ornaments around their necks (Judges 6:1–5; 8:21, 26).

Now, about those humps: camels do not store water in them. They are not giant sponges. That hump is made up of fat—

stored energy, like the Energizer Bunny—that allows them to keep going and going and going when every other animal drops over dead in the desert.

Get Stronger

God always made a point of reminding the Israelites that horses, as great of a battle weapon as they were, were not what won the war. Relying on God's help was what got the job done. You see, you may win some battles with strong horses, but what happens when the other guys have more horses and chariots than you do? It's the same today. We need to trust God for everything. Money, jobs, friends, good times, and even happiness all come and go, but God will always, always be there for us!

EXTRAORDINARY ANIMALS

Talking Snake Tells a Lie

Remember the serpent that lied to Eve in the garden of Eden? When God first created snakes he said they were good (Genesis 1:24–25). This one went astray. Did you ever wonder how the snake managed to talk? Genesis 3:1 says "the serpent was more crafty that any of the wild animals," so possibly snakes used to be some kind of big-brained beings. Either that or "crafty serpent" means the Devil himself, so the Devil possessed a snake and talked through him like a puppet. Makes you wonder though why Eve didn't interrupt the conversation with, "Hey! You're a snake. You're only supposed to hiss or rattle!"

Time We Had a Talk

Balaam liked to brag what a great prophet he was. "Yeah, man, I don't needa close my eyes! I see visions with my eyes open." Better get your eyes checked, dude! There's one angry angel with a sword in front of you. If Balaam's donkey hadn't seen the angel and stopped, Balaam would've been dead meat. Balaam still didn't get it, so God had to give his donkey the gift of speech, and she had a long overdue talk with him. They covered everything: her work record, his bad temper, everything.

"Then the Lord opened the donkey's mouth, and she said to Balaam, 'What have I done to you to make you beat me these three times?' Balaam answered the donkey, 'You have made a fool of me! If I had a sword in my hand, I would kill you right now.' The donkey said to Balaam, 'Am I not your own donkey, which you have always ridden, to this day? Have I been in the habit of doing this to you?' 'No,' he said. Then the Lord opened Balaam's eyes, and he saw the angel of the Lord standing in the road with his sword drawn. So he bowed low and fell facedown" (Numbers 22:21–33).

Animal Teachers

When Job's wise pals told him really obvious stuff, he replied, "Who does not know all these things?" Then he told them to get clued in. "Ask the animals, and they will teach you, or the birds of the air, and they will tell you ... or let the fish of the sea inform you" (Job 2:7–8). Can't you picture these wise guys looking at each other, saying, "He's joking, right?"

Milk Cows in the Sun House

Bethshemesh means "House of the Sun," but when two milk cows headed up the road for Bethshemesh one day they were not heading for the tanning salon. Nope! These walking milk jugs were pulling a cart, and on that cart was none other than the ark of the covenant. The amazing thing was, milk cows will never willingly leave their calves. But these cows did. Why? Because God told them to take the ark to Bethshemesh (1 Samuel 6:7–12).

Man-Killing Lion Has Weird Day

Here's a lion that got his orders from God. He's out minding his business one day, not even hungry, and suddenly along comes a disobedient prophet on a donkey. Lionel roars, pulls the prophet off the donkey, and kills him right there. The donkey is cool as a pickle: he doesn't run away, and the lion just sits there by the dead prophet. The donkey's standing there. The lion's sitting there. Everybody's like, okay, now what? Finally an old prophet comes along. He looks at the lion. He looks at the donkey. Then he loads the dead guy on the donkey and leaves. Then the lion gets up and goes on his way. And the whole town is thinking, "Man, that was weird." You've got to read this one (1 Kings 13)!

Lions Pass up Tasty Prophet

Okay, another lion story—only in this story the lions are hungry right out of their brains. The prophet Daniel was living in Babylon and some powerful dudes were jealous of him and the great relationship he had with the king, so they tricked the king into passing a law that no one could worship God or they'd be lion lunch. Daniel keeps praying, gets caught, and in he goes to the lion's den. The next morning the king runs up and asks if Daniel's okay. Daniel says, "My God sent his angel, and he shut the mouths of the lions." So then the king throws Daniel's enemies in and the angel's, like, no longer there. You can guess what happened (Daniel 6). Daniel made it through to the morning. His enemies didn't even make it down to the floor.

Ravenous Ravaging Ravens

When you think of animals bringing you food you might picture a hunting dog with a duck in its mouth. But when Elijah was hiding out in a canyon, God had a flock of ravens (bigger and uglier than crows) drop out of the sky with Elijah's breakfast and dinner (1 King 17:2–6). Elijah had to be mighty hungry to take the food from their dirty beaks. You see, ravens generally eat dead animals. Proverbs 30:17 says they're particularly crazy about eyeballs. Gulp!

Monster-Fish Ocean Cruise

When Jonah disobeyed God and was chucked in the ocean, he was swallowed by one humongous fish. This might've been one of those weird-looking monsters from the ocean depths, like the last of his species. It could also have been a whale shark. There are several recorded instances where fisherman have been swallowed by a whale shark and have lived to tell the story. Whatever he was, fisho was on a mission for God. He showed up right on cue, gulped Jonah down (that had to be scary!), then swam around the ocean for three days and nights. Finally, when it still couldn't digest Jonah—and Jonah had repented—God sent the fish to land where it surfaced, puked Jonah up alive, then headed back out to sea.

Try That Again Next Year!

When the tax collectors asked Peter, "Doesn't your teacher pay the temple tax?" Peter said, "Yes." Jesus overheard, stopped Peter at the door, then told him to go fishing. He was to look in the mouth of the first fish he caught and he'd find a four-drachma coin—enough to pay his and Peter's tax. So Peter looked and there it was (Matthew 17:24–27). Wow! Try that again next tax season. Fact

is, there's a fish in the Sea of Galilee called the Tilapia that carries its eggs in its big mouth. The coin must've been its nest egg. (If you don't get the pun, a "nest egg" means saved-up money.)

GeT SMaRTeR

God has used animals in some very cool and unusual ways to help and teach people. But the main way he wants to bless others is through people. That's part of loving one another. God wants to use you. Pray and tell God that you're available and then look for opportunities to help. And you can't say, "God can't use me. I don't know enough."—Or any other excuse. If he can use "dumb" animals he can use any of us.

amazing unreal creatures

INTRODUCTION

If an animal doesn't even exist, then what is it doing in the Bible? Well, God loves to teach us lessons using real animals—but when the lessons get too wild and a real animal just won't do, that's when he brings on the four-headed leopards, seven-headed dragons, one-horned goats, and talking thistles.

Besides, when you're trying to get a point across and you use real animals, halfway through your parable people may wonder, "Is this guy actually talking about animals or is this a parable or what?" But if you say, "I saw a seven-headed dragon rise up out of the sea," right away everyone sits up, grabs their popcorn, and gets ready for a parable. They know they're going to get a real show. So these creatures of visions may be wilder than wild, but there's a point to them.

A vision, by the way, was when God's Spirit showed a prophet pictures of something. The prophet saw this "vision" with his spiritual eyes or in his mind—not with his natural eyes. Prophets often had visions with their eyes closed, sometimes when they were asleep, but other times when they were going about their daily business with their eyes wide open. Suddenly "heaven would open" and it was like this other dimension appeared in front of them.

One last thing: there are also mythological animals like unicorns and gryphons that somehow ended up by mistake in the King James version of the Bible. These critters don't exist and shouldn't even be there. But they're such common creatures in today's fantasy stories and animated videos that we thought you'd like to hear about the times they're mentioned in the good old King James Version of the Bible, and why.

WILD CREATURES IN DREAMS AND VISIONS

Crocodile Cows

Cows eat grass, right? Then they flop down, belch up the half-digested sludge, and—Ho hum! Booooring!—chew it all over again. Well, there were seven ugly, skinny cows that must've been burping and chewing plenty to digest what they ate! They were out for a swim in the Nile River, worked up one enormous big appetite, then rushed up into the reeds and attacked and ate

seven big fat cows! (Can't you just see the reeds thrashing and cow parts flying?) Yes, these were cows—not crocodiles, not velociraptors. Okay, okay, relax, it was only a dream that God gave to Pharaoh, king of Egypt. Whew! But scary! Joseph interpreted the dream for Pharaoh and put God's plan in place to save the world from starvation (Genesis 41:1–4). Cool.

Cute Li'l Man-Killer Cubs

Ezekiel told a parable about a lioness that taught her cubs to hunt—only she taught them how to kill and eat people! Naughty, naughty. But her first cub was trapped in a pit and taken away. So what'd she do? She trained another man-killing cub. This lion was like Super Lion. He was so strong he broke down fortresses and devastated towns. The whole countryside was terrified when he roared. ("It's a cat, it's a lion, no, it's Super Lion!") But wouldn't you know it: they threw nets on him and trapped him in a pit too (Ezekiel 19:1–9).

This one had you going, I bet. You probably thought it was really about real lions until Power Paw started batting down buildings and bull-dozing cities. So what was this about? Lion cub number one was weak King Jehoahaz, who, was carried off to Egypt. Lion number two was stronger King Zedekiah, who was carried off to Babylon.

The Flyin' Lion

About 3000 B.C. the Babylonians invented a god who was basically a regular lion type—except that he had eagle's wings. He was a symbol of power and majesty and kings, and of course, he could fly. The winged lion was common in Babylonian mythology. When God wanted to give Daniel a vision that the Babylonian king, Belshazzar, could understand, he described Babylon as a flying lion (Daniel 7:4). Can't you just see the king raising his hand and waving frantically? "Oh! Oh! I know! The winged lion is Babylon! Right?" Riiiight.

The Great Hunchback Bear

One night Daniel had a vision about a shaggy old bear raised up on one side like the hunchbacked bear of Notre Dame. It had three ribs between its teeth (Daniel 7:5). Now what on earth does this mean? Well, the mountains of Media and Persia were full of bears and to the Babylonians, the rough mountain people were like bears. This bear  was the Empire of the Medes and the Persians, and since the Persians were stronger than the Medes, their side was "raised up." And the three ribs? They were the three great nations the Medo-Persians had conquered: Lydia, Babylon, and Egypt.

Four-Headed Leopard

When God wanted to tell Daniel about
Alexander the Great and the Greek empire, and
how fast they would conquer the known world,
he gave Daniel a dream about a leopard with
four wings and four heads (Daniel 7:6). The
leopard was Greece. Leopards are fast—and
with wings, even faster. The leopard symbolized
Alexander the Great conquering the world in
ten years. And the four heads? After Alexander
died, his four generals divided up his empire. It
happened just like God showed Daniel it would.

The Utterly Awesome Lamb

John is in heaven looking on the throne of God
when suddenly this little lamb walks up. Now,
normally little lambs don't have horns. They
have to grow up into big tough rams for that.
Another thing is, they usually have only two
horns. Some of the more exotic rams have four
horns and seven eyes. Just when John is won-
dering what this lamb is, everyone starts singing
praise to it! Turns out he's Jesus! Relax, this wild
look is only symbolic (Revelation 5:6–14).

The fact that he was a "little lamb" (*arnion* in
Greek) shows that he was pure and innocent.
But he wasn't weak. In the Bible, horns symbol-
ize power, and Jesus had lots of that! And seven
eyes? That symbolizes the all-knowing power of
God's Spirit.

Ram-Horned Dragon Beast

Jesus said false prophets were like wolves disguised as sheep (Matthew 7:15). But this next guy takes the cake! He was a dragon disguised as a sheep! One day John saw this wannabe-sheep in a vision rising right up out of the ground like some swamp monster coming out of the bog. He had two horns like a sheep, fine and well, but when he opened his mouth he didn't make any sweet little baaaa-baaa sounds. It was a dragon roaring. Think T-Rex sound effects. False prophet? Oh yeah. This creature

represents THE False Prophet who gets the world to worship the Antichrist (Revelation 13:11–14). He'll look and act peaceful enough like a sheep, but underneath the Devil will be at work.

Get Deeper

If someone had a vision about you, what kind of beast or creature do you think God would use to represent who you really are and what your heart is like? Jesus told a story about some people whom he described as sheep and some who were goats. The sheep were people who did what God wanted them to do and were rewarded. The goats didn't and didn't get rewarded. You can read about it in Matthew 25:31–46.

Fantastic, Fictional Beings

Unicorns

Unicorns are mentioned nine times in the King James Version of the Bible. (This is the English translation published by authority of James I, King of England, in 1611.) Numbers 23:22 says, "He hath ... the strength of a unicorn." King James believed in unicorns, but since no one has ever seen one, the translators of the New International Version realized that the Hebrew word *reem* meant aurochs, a powerful, six-foot-high wild ox. From the side it looked like it had one horn. And the side is the place to be. You do not want to stand in front of one of these bruisers. (Well, no need to worry. They're extinct now.)

There was one unicorn in the Bible, though it was a goat not a horse—and it was only a vision, not a real animal. Daniel saw a goat with a prominent horn between his eyes attack a big-horned ram. The shaggy goat symbolized Greece and the large horn between its eyes was Alexander the Great who would conquer the known world (Daniel 7:5–8,21–22). Is that weird or what? This vision was fulfilled 220 years later.

Flying White Horses

The ancient Greeks believed in a flying horse with wings called Pegasus. The Bible says nothing about horses with wings but—surprise! It does talk about magnificent, white flying horses. For real! In the Battle of Armageddon Jesus will come out of the sky riding a white horse and so will the armies of heaven (Revelation 19:11–14). Flying horses? That's enough to make a horse-lover out of anyone.

Of course, some heavenly horses would be a bit too hot to ride. When Elijah was carried up to heaven in a whirlwind, "a chariot of fire and horses of fire appeared." Years later, Elisha and his servant saw "horses and chariots of fire" around the city of Dothan (2 Kings 2:11; 6:17). If the horses are made out of fire, you'd really be sitting on the hot seat if you tried to ride them.

Satyrs—Half Man, Half Goat

In Greek myths, a satyr was a weird god with a human upper body and goat's back half and legs and horns. Satyrs loved to get drunk and dance. Did they exist? In the King James Version of the Bible, Isaiah 13:21 says, "Their houses shall be full of doleful creatures ... and satyrs shall dance there." The Hebrew word, *sair* actually means goat, so the translators of the New International Version decided, "Hey, since sair actually means goat, let's translate it goat." So they did. (Question: so why did the KJV scholars translate sair as satyrs? Because a couple times sair also means "goat god" so the translators thought, "Hey! The satyr was a goat god.")

Cockatrice? Flying Fiery Serpents?

According to Greek legends the cockatrice was a bizarre beast—half rooster (cock) and half snake. Cockatrice is mentioned four times in the King James Bible. Isaiah 14:29 gives a parable, saying, "Out of the serpent's root shall come forth a cockatrice, and his fruit shall be a fiery flying serpent." (See, back in 1611 they believed in cockatrices and flying serpents.) The NIV translates this verse: "From the root of that snake will spring up a viper, its fruit will be a darting, venomous serpent." You guessed it: this is no poisonous rooster, just a regular, everyday deadly viper. And those "fiery flying serpents" aren't baby dragons. Just venomous serpents. Hooo-eeee! It wasn't just the "thees" and the "thous" in the King James Bible that confused people.

Gryphons are Detestable!

The ancient Greeks believed in the gryps, a monstrous mythological beast half eagle, half lion. We call these imaginary creatures gryphons. The Jews knew these Greek myths and believed there was some truth to them, so when they translated the Law from Hebrew into Greek, they translated *peres* (bone breaker) as gryps instead of vulture. So Leviticus 11:13 reads: "These are the birds you are to detest and not eat ... the eagle, the gryphon, the black vulture ..." Since gryphons didn't exist, it was easy for Jewish people to not eat them.

Get Smarter

Why did the ancient Jewish translators—and even Christians hundreds of years ago—still believe in unicorns, cockatrices, satyrs, gryphons, and dragons? Well, they hadn't even begun to explore the world back then and there were still lots of unknown monsters around. It's only been in the last few centuries that scientists and Bible translators have sorted out what actually existed, and what didn't. The Bible is God's Word and it's been accurately preserved. But we don't have photographs and dictionaries from Bible times, so some of the facts about food, animals, geography, weapons, and other cultural things have been more accurately understood and translated as we've learned more about those times through archaeological discoveries.

DRAGONS— ARE THEY REAL?

For thousands of years people have believed in dragons. But are they real or myth? Or something in between—like, you know, maybe leftover dinosaurs with severe gas? Come with us as we explore the strange world that may or may not be inhabited by dragons. You judge.

In the King James Version, Micah 1:8 reads, "I will make a wailing like the dragons." Dragons are mentioned twenty-one times in the King James translation of the Old Testament. Obviously King James was one big dragon fan. However, the translators of the New International Version realized that *tannim* actually meant howlers, and that these howlers lived in the desert with owls and other beasts, so they

were jackals. You know, wild dogs that hunt in packs.

Of the thirty-three times dragons are mentioned in the KJV Bible, fourteen times it's actually talking about jackals; seven times it means a sea serpent. For example, Egypt was an enemy of God's people, so God pictured her as a great sea monster, "Leviathan the gliding serpent, Leviathan the coiling serpent ... the monster of the sea." (Ezekiel 29:3; Psalm 74:13–14; Isaiah 27:1).

Symbolic? Real? Well, there are real sea monsters. There are huge crocodiles in the Nile, not to mention whales and 55-foot, ten-armed giant squids in the ocean. "There is the sea ... teeming with living things ... and the leviathan, which you formed to frolic there" (Psalm 104:26).

And hey, let's talk about this sea monster, leviathan. In Job 41 God spends an entire

chapter talking about some huge beast named leviathan dragging its big old self through a swamp, and it's anybody's guess what that is. Some people say it's just a giant crocodile, but seriously, a croc that gets hit by iron spears and asks, "Who's throwing straw at me?" (Job 41:26–29) Sounds more like Godzilla on four legs. God told Job, "flames dart from his mouth" (Job 41:18–21). Now that may be just symbolic, but that is where legends of fire-breathing dragons come from.

Okay, so lots of so-called dragons were simply jackals or some kind of weird water monsters. But what about the twelve times dragons are mentioned in the book of Revelation? John talked about a great red dragon (Revelation 12) but this dragon is symbolic. For one thing, he has seven—count 'em, seven—heads and golden crowns on his heads. (And you think the cartoons stretch it when they show a multi-headed dragon?) Okay, so it's not a real beast here on earth. But the symbolism has a point: that dragon was a symbol of evil. As Revelation 12:9 says, "The great dragon was hurled down—the ancient serpent called the Devil, or Satan."

So do dragons exist? Well, they exist in myths. They exist as symbols. And they certainly exist in movies. But if you mean are there really giant four-footed lizards with pterodactyl wings, breathing out fire? Nuh uh.

GET SMARTER

Whether the creature was inspired by some dinosaur of ancient times or the visions that God gave to his prophets, God still dreamed up the dragon, just like when we draw an imaginary creature on a piece of paper. God has blessed us with creative gifts as well, and he wants us to have fun using our imagination and creating. If you like to write, pull out a piece of paper and write a story about an amazing creature made up from your own imagination. If you like to draw, draw one! And if your parents ask you what you're doing, let them know you're being creative like God.

talking plant creatures

Talking Plants

Maybe your grandmother talks to her plants as she walks around with a watering can. You know, stuff like: "Oh! And how are you petunias this morning? Are you daffodils happy? Are you thirsty? There, you little dears! That should do you." But unless Grandma is living in a VeggieTales® video, no way are the plants going to talk back to her. But in the Bible, people liked to tell stories about talking plants and weird veggie creatures. David talked about happy trees that sang and Ezekiel talked about trees that were green with envy. Everyone

understood that they were telling stories to get a point across. They weren't creatures that grew from some strange alien spore carried on a meteor to earth. And they weren't saying that plants actually talked. (It's really, really important that you understand that or the following stories will completely weird you out.)

The Thistle Who Got Stomped

Jehoash, king of Israel, told this short story: "A thistle in Lebanon sent a message to a cedar in Lebanon, 'Give your daughter to my son in marriage.' Then a wild beast in Lebanon came along and trampled the thistle underfoot" (2 Kings 14:9). And that was it. Ummm ... thanks Jehoash. It was really, like, nice of you to tell that story, but, ah, we're just dying to know: did little Thistle Boy ever marry two-ton Cedar Girl? You can't tell us? Well, can you tell us what this story means then? Oh that. Sure! Amaziah, king of Judah, had just defeated the Edomites and was so proud about how big and tough he was that he challenged Jehoash, king of Israel, to battle. Jehoash was basically telling him: "You are the dinky little thistle. I am the monster cedar. Mess with me and you'll get stomped."

Long Live King Thistle!

Here's a story about a talking thorn bush. Talking thorn and thistle tales were apparently

very popular in the Middle East back then. The story goes like this: the trees go out walking to find a king to rule over them. First they come to the olive tree. "Be our king," they beg. But Oliver isn't willing, so the trees keep walking. Next they ask the fig tree, but Figgy says, "Nuh-uh. I got a good thing going with my sweet figs." By this time the trees are getting worried. They ask the vine, but Vine is, like, loaded down with grapes. Finally all the trees say to the thorn bush, "Come and be our king." You know they're getting desperate by this time. Thorny says sure. But he says it with style. He tells them, "Sure I'll be your king IF all you trees can fit under my shade." All the trees had to do was look down at the pitiful shade he gave and realize he was not going to be much of a king.

Jotham, the last son of Gideon, told the men of Shechem this parable when they were about to make Abimelech their king. He was basically mocking them for being so desperate that they were willing to make a worthless man their king. It gets worse. Jothan said that fire was going to come out of the thorn bush and burn all the trees down (Judges 9:1–20). They didn't listen to Jotham's parable. They made Abimelech king, and Bim ended up killing thousands of them later on.

Worship Trees Rock Out!

There's a couple of ways that vegetation and even rocks can say something without talking. Did you know that trees sing and clap their hands? Well, symbolically at least. Isaiah said, "The mountains and hills will burst into song before you, and all the trees of the field will clap their hands" (Isaiah 55:12).

When we look at the huge, majestic mountains, the wonderful trees, and how everything works perfectly together in God's creation, it all shows us how great God the Creator is. Paul said that we know there is a God by looking at his creation (Romans 1:19–20). So in that way the trees, flowers, and mountains are all speaking to us and giving glory to God.

David said, "Then the trees of the forest will sing, they will sing for joy before the Lord" (1 Chronicles 16:33). If you really hear a tree singing, well, chances are someone put their radio in the branches or they're stuck up there themselves.

Another way veggies can talk to us is that God created things to work according to his order—so by looking at parts of God's creation we can "hear" with our eyes things about God and life.

Jesus pointed out that the lilies of the field didn't labor at a job or spin cloth, but it wasn't

like his disciples thought they did. Jesus wasn't saying lilies were lazy either. His point was that they didn't sweat to make their own clothes, yet "not even Solomon in all his splendor was dressed like one of these. If that is how God clothes the grass of the field ... will he not much more clothe you?" (Matthew 6:28–30) Every time we look at a flower it should remind us of how God takes care of us. And that is how lilies can talk.

Wheat Bows Down

In the old days farmers would cut down grain with hand sickles, then tie them in bundles called sheaves and stand them up for the sun to dry. Well, once Joseph and his ten brothers were tying grain in sheaves when Joseph's sheave rose and stood upright all by itself. This surprised Joseph, but what really blew his mind was when all his brothers' sheaves came waddling over, gathered around his sheave, and bowed down. Then Joseph woke up. Whew! Just a dream! (Genesis 37:5–8) But the dream

was from God and he was using veggies again to tell Joseph that he would eventually rule over his brothers. Which, of course, is exactly what happened.

Envious Trees of Eden

You'd think the trees in the garden of Eden would be the most majestic, beautiful trees going, right? But in Ezekiel 31:2–16 God told a parable about the kingdom of Assyria. He said Assyria was "once a cedar in Lebanon with beautiful branches. No tree in the garden of God could match its beauty." It was "the envy of all the trees of Eden." Then the Assyrian cedar became vain. It became proud of its height so God let it get cut down. Then all the trees of Eden were consoled. "Well, we don't look so ugly-wulgly anymore now that Cedar-boy got the ax."

God was telling this story to the Egyptians. They were proud of their great strength. They were sure they could defeat the Babylonians. But God reminded them that the powerful Assyrian empire had thought the same thing: they were greater than all other nations (trees), but now even they had been defeated. God was saying, "If even the biggest, best, and most beautiful got axed, don't you be proud."

It's a Wheat-Eat-Wheat World

Picture this: Seven healthy heads of grain are growing on a single stalk. That's kind of strange, but at least they're healthy. Then suddenly seven thin, scorched heads of grain sprout up and—gulp—swallow up (!) the seven healthy heads. What is this? A Venus flytrap in the wheat field? A bizarre sci-fi movie? The result of DNA tampering? Relax. It was God giving Pharaoh a dream that seven years of famine were coming (Genesis 41:5–7; 25–31). Oh! Is that all?

Almond Blossom Snake

Once in a while scientists discover some new thingie that's neither plant nor animal, but here we have something that was both. Well, kind of. Aaron had this amazing wooden staff. One time he threw it down and it turned into a snake (Exodus 7:8–10). Another time he left it lying in God's tent overnight and it budded, blossomed, and produced almonds (Numbers 17:8). Cool! Granted, this almond tree couldn't talk, but at one point it did have a brain and hissed. God used a veggie that wasn't even alive anymore, a dead stick, and did some amazing stuff with it.

Trees That Tell Fortunes?

The pagan Canaanites were highly superstitious. They believed that certain ancient trees could reveal the future. There was a particularly famous one mentioned in the Bible, the "great tree of Moreh at Shechem" known as the soothsayer's tree (Genesis 12:5; Judges 9:7). How did this oak tree supposedly reveal the future? Probably when its leaves rustled in the wind, the Canaanites would interpret what it sounded like: "Wow! Did you hear that? The tree just said I should be king!" "Oh! And listen now! It's giving the winning lottery numbers!" Ha. This is one way vegetation does not talk.

In the Bible God used trees, thistles, thorn bushes, wheat sheaves, and other vegetation in different ways to get his point across. (Today he seems to be using cucumbers, tomatoes, and asparagus a lot.)

Get Smarter

talking veggie creatures, animals of all sorts, seven-headed dragons, and much more. God dreamed them all up, even the ones in visions and parables that don't really exist. (Or at least don't exist on earth.) And he created all these plants and animals for him and for us—to help us, to feed us, for us to enjoy, and for us to learn from. And the greatest thing we can learn from them all is just how cool and awesome God is! He's a phenomenal Creator and a loving and caring Father to his children. But he's also God, the Creator and all-powerful, all-knowing owner of all he has created. Our response? We need to thank him for his creation, get to know him, and receive his love and care as our Heavenly Father, and follow and obey him (with the help of his Spirit and grace) as our Lord and our God.

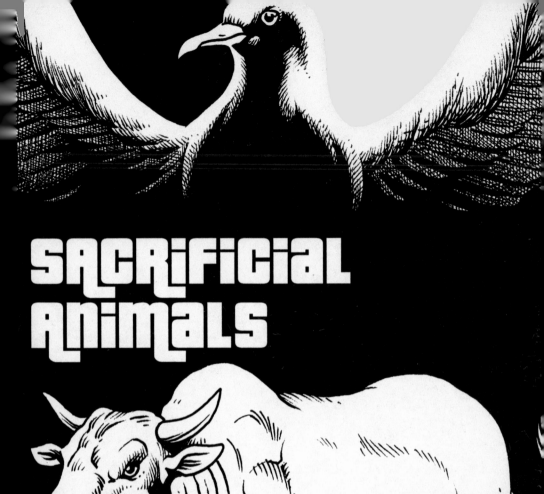

SACRIFICIAL ANIMALS

SACRRIFICING ANIMALS

In the Old Testament when someone sinned, they would sacrifice an animal to God on a stack of stones called an altar. This animal was usually a sheep, a goat, or a bull, and taking its life helped people understand that sin was serious and that a price had to be paid to make things right with God. They did not eat the meat of a "sin offering," but most offerings were eaten.

The first recorded sacrifice in the Bible was when Abel offered God a lamb from his flock (Genesis 4:3–4). After Abel, Noah sacrificed all kinds of animals and birds (Genesis 8:20), and after him we see Abraham sacrificing a heifer, a goat, a ram, a dove, and a pigeon.

Then Abraham stood by and chased off the buzzards that came to eat the meat (Genesis 15:9–11).

Oxen Barbeques

Besides sin offerings, the Israelites also had

fellowship offerings. These symbolized peace between God and man. The fun part was afterward when they cut up the meat and had a big old happy barbeque. They could enjoy the meat of a thank offering. Cattle, goats, or sheep could be offered, but most of the time people sacrificed either a ram or an ox. An ox is a bull that's been castrated, and if you don't know what that means, look it up in the dictionary. (Hint: no new little bulls or cows will be calling him "Daddy" after that.)

The Escape-Goat Escapes

When something goes wrong and one person gets all the blame—even though it wasn't all their fault or their fault at all—they're called a "scapegoat." This comes from the Israelite Day of Atonement where the high priest sacrificed one goat, then put his hands on the head of the other goat, confessed the nation's sins, and put them on the goat's head. ("Whoa! Why do I suddenly have a headache?") Then the goat was driven into the wilderness. The first goat was killed, this one escaped, so he was called the 'scape-goat' (Leviticus 16:6–10; 21–22).

Dos Doves Will Do

According to the Law of Moses, after a woman gave birth she was to offer a year-old lamb and a pigeon or dove as a purification offering. If she was poor, she could offer two doves (Leviticus 12). Apparently Mary and Joseph were poor because after Jesus was born, they offered two doves (Luke 2:22–24).

Sheep Top the List

Sheep, lambs, rams, you name it, these wooly wonders were at the top of the list when it came to animals that were sacrificed. The Jewish Passover was really no day to be a sheep. Not that any day was, actually. But on Passover, in just one night, nearly half a million sheep died. (They were all eaten, of course.) The upside to this is that lambs symbolized salvation and they were the most important item in the most important national feast (Exodus 12:1–14).

The <u>Best</u> I Said! Not the <u>Worst</u>!

When the Jews brought an animal to the temple to sacrifice, they were to bring the best they had, an animal "without defect" (Leviticus 9:3). But in Malachi's day, people were keeping the best and offering God diseased animals. Like, God noticed. " 'When you bring injured, crippled or diseased animals and offer them as sacrifices, should I accept them from your hands?' says the Lord. 'Try offering them to your governor! Would he be pleased with you?' " (Malachi 1:8, 13) Not.

Perfectly Perfect Lambs

In Jesus' day the high priests had a racket going. Since they were the final authority on whether or not a sacrifice was "without blemish," whenever anyone brought an animal to be sacrificed, the priests would look and look until they found some tiny, eensy blemish, then say, "Sorry! Reject! You'll have to buy one of ours—for a high price." This is why Jesus kicked over these robbers' tables, made a whip, and drove them out of the temple (John 2:13–16).

112,000,000 Quarter-Pounders Coming Up!

When King Solomon opened the brand new temple, he sacrificed 22,000 cattle and 120,000 sheep and goats in fellowship offerings (1 Kings

8:62–63). That's barrels and barrels of blood everywhere! The priests must've been splattered from head to toe. Bet no amount of washing got their robes clean. And who ate all that meat? If you figure 1,000 pounds of meat from each bull and 50 pounds of meat from each goat or sheep, that's 22,000,000 pounds of beef and 6,000,000 pounds of goat/lamb. "All Israel" was with Solomon, and 6,000,000 Israelites with an appetite means every person had to eat nearly nineteen Quarter-pounders. Burp! Good thing the celebration lasted a while. "Another McSheep, please!"

Second Biggest Bash

In King Hezekiah's day one Passover feast was so successful that the whole assembly then agreed to celebrate the festival seven more days. Hey! Party on! Hezekiah sent 1,000 bulls and 7,000 sheep and goats to the barbeque spits, and the officials threw in an additional 1,000 bulls and 10,000 sheep and goats (2 Chronicles 30:23–24). "Hey! C'mon, people! There's still lots of food!"

Burning Cow Dung

When a bull was sacrificed as a sin offering, the entire bull then had to be burned to ashes—the meat, hide, head, legs, guts, and offal (dung) (Leviticus 4:11). Of course, burning cow dung was nothing new for the Israelites. They often gathered dry cow dung and burned it as fuel to cook their food over (Ezekiel 4:15). ("Mmmmm! Zesty flavor! What'd you cook this over? Goat dung?" "No, just regular bull poop.")

GET DEEPER

The Bible says that the penalty for sin is death. But no person on earth could die for someone else's sins because they had to die for their own. Animal sacrifice then became the symbol for something innocent dying to pay the price for sin. But it took Jesus' death to really do the job. He was God's Son and lived without sinning—he could therefore die in our place and pay the price for sin. That's why the Bible says that Jesus is the Lamb of God, a lamb without blemish or defect. There is no need for sacrificing animals today because Jesus paid the price for every sin anyone had ever committed or would ever commit. He was the ultimate sacrifice.

PRAYER

If you believe in Jesus then one day you'll go to the most awesome paradise imaginable. In fact, heaven even defies imagination! "No eye has seen, no ear has heard, no mind has conceived what God has prepared for those who love him" (1 Corinthians 2:9). Heaven is not only full of fantastic new stuff, but lots of fantastic creatures we know from earth such as lions, horses, leopards, etc.—now beautiful and perfect forever! And if you love Jesus, you'll be there too! If you haven't accepted Jesus yet and you want to be God's child, sincerely say this prayer:

"Dear God, I know I'm a sinner. I've made wrong choices and done bad things. I'm very sorry. Please forgive me. I know your Son, Jesus, died for my sins. I believe that you raised him from the dead. I accept what he did for me and receive him as my Lord. Help me trust and obey you and make right choices. Thanks for loving me, living in me, and making me your child. In Jesus' name, Amen."

zonder**kidz**.

We want to hear from you. Please send your comments
about this book to us in care of zreview@zondervan.com. Thank you.

Grand Rapids, MI 49530
www.zonderkidz.com

ZONDERVAN.com/
AUTHORTRACKER
follow your favorite authors